Rules of the House

D1604438

Rules of the House

—

Tsering Wangmo Dhompa

Tsering Wangmo Dhompa

Apogee Press
Berkeley · California
2002

For Tsering Choden Dhompa
Beloved mother

Grateful acknowledgments to: *6ix, #135, A.bacus, Atlanta Review, Bongos of the Lord, California Quarterly, Coffee Eyed Review, Fourteen Hills, International Poetry Review, Mid-American Review, Mungo Vs. Ranger, Tangram Press, Transfer* and *Visions International*.

Thanks also to Cid Corman, Myung Mi Kim, Anne Waldman, Kabir M. Heimsath, Elaine Seiler, Melvin Shaffer, Val and Maush.

Book design by Philip Krayna Design, Berkeley, California.
www.pkdesign.net

ISBN 0-9669937-9-9. Library of Congress Catalog Card Number 2002111906.

Published by Apogee Press, Post Office Box 8177, Berkeley CA, 94707-8177.
www.apogeepress.com

Table of Contents

As remembered

I am only beginning to understand how seasons affect me.

Winter. Snow beating street people into obedience. How mothers held back from stepping out in discreetly ornamented shoes and thin nylon socks.

This is the way I count years: the winters we had fire and the summers we erased because we were in another place.

I am told I was five in 1971 even though my birth certificate states I was born in 1969. The elders count on their fingers. They have done it for a long time.

It was winter but not the kind of winter they were born into. They were wearing hand knitted woolen sweaters. I was wearing a jacket that children born to refugees wear.

When I am with them, I cannot say I remember. I say, as I am told I remember.

It is not the accuracy of the story that concerns us.

But who gets to tell it.

(i)

They took their lungs
to water – thinking river,
spring, alpine lake.
When the wind came
it was like being
in the mountains. Hull
hoisted far away.
A journey begun.

Since

Spring was late. We watched her toss her seeds like a weary pilgrim. The jacaranda flowered a hazy purple and the hermit said it would be a good year. He said chewing nettle leaves was a thing of the past.

Hermits too need to keep up with the times.

Dreams culled for the lama. We offer him purple petals, ask him to translate sorrow, lighten karma. A snap of fingers and we congeal to fate.

He changes reality into illusion by scoffing at it. We wander in the bazaar in a daze then realize we are dizzy because we are seeing too much.

Dust prisms in noon-day brilliance. Light sheltered in street corners.

At the end of the meeting, we touch foreheads and bless each other. *Ga Sho* May you be loved.

The eyes of the stupa trapped in rain while around it monsters are torn down and reborn as rashes on the landscape.

Through the endless yawn of feet, *Om Mani Padme Hum* (this too is translated).

Pigeon droppings in scalp. We return to the lama, teach us something we can remember.

Let your hair grow. Give eyes to your feet. Don't. Follow.

First lesson

Men love
silence in women

said aunt Pema.
Use fingers to count

the years of the sun.
Graze lips against its first advance.

When tea is cold,
allow to spill.

What comes warm
is good warm.

The right hand kneads barley.
Left washes your bottom.

The rest
is fate.

write needs   elasticity
slices   in the mouth
leftist farmers   pertinent wedges
              four 2 inch nails

In the event of change

I am saying primroses lined the pathway of toothless hedges.

I am saying the ocean shimmered like corrugated steel in the morning sun.

The context of my story changes when you enter. Then I am dung on the wall of the nomad's field. Then the everyday waking person.

I am nodding in your direction like fissures between dandelion fur. Seeing in your manner.

I am speaking your pace. Slippage of silk slippers.

I say you are losing sight. I say your breasts are dry shells.

I am afraid of what I am capable of doing.

This is all a manner of stating how I prepare myself to be loved.

Cutting the cloth

In pieces we think. Wording eyes.

How we see when sun splinters enter.

Her laugh. When the river ran full,

we lapped it up. Her laugh; when she did

that gurgling of tea on coal.

How should I explain. We lived

by a water tank. It was easy to speak.

Restless in light-scorched air

(her words for heat).

Restless ears we pressed against cold

steel, and bartered tales.

(ii)

Not until
a way is found
to talk about us.
Not like this.
Not confining
the look
when wings
carved in the sand
found motions
of their own.

My people are from the mountains. They have other qualities and
are not ashamed to call each other "my people."

The opening day

When the gutters spill open, we throw ourselves in. Pink dyes from the carpet factory alter the texture of water. We splash pink on the road.

Everyday is a new colour.

M suggests our pomegranate tree be an offering to all sentient beings. Someone, F says, had better benefit from such stupidity. He has plans for the fruits he will pluck.

Three fruits drop to the ground in the first week of rain.

Pink umbrellas are on sale. F gets one for the girls.

The evening light falls ripe and round on the fruits. A crimson rests on the waist of the tree.

Tashi shaved her head and said she was ready to collect rain as the monsoon took many jabs at us.

The elder cannot decide whether rain is a good thing. Farmers are happy, she said, and they are used to being wet. The newspaper ran a story on rice fields and farming festivals.

Too much rain is said to crush celebrations.

The earth takes the best (said the elder).

When the monsoons are over, Tashi wants to take her to the zoo.

Sun storm

Like brides behind veils, my people peep from drawn curtains and feel the air with their fingers. They do not see any use for heat and are not hospitable to it. Electric fans focus on bare shoulder blades and erect nipples.

Mosquitoes persist. Hands do not move fast enough.

On arrival, my people were instructed to throw away their black clothes, then taught to distract the sun. In crisp white pajamas and khadi shirts, they walked the camp till it paled to a canvas of gathering spirits.

Night led them to the edge of the stream. Feet in water, they talked about what they had left to lose.

Some afternoons, old stories were translated into Tibetan. *You are blessed*, strangers said. *God has delivered you. Such is his bountiful nature.*

Sparrows tattooed the air. Prayer beads clicked as mantras circulated above the parable of a son who erred and was forgiven. The story teller's lips bent with crystals of sweat.

Jesus loves you. For years, F thought Jesus was the president of a country. He thought he was a rich old man.

He told one story-telling woman she was wrong. Jesus had nothing to do with it. It was all fate.

Second lesson

The newspaper showed a boy drinking from the sky. Water rested in his clavicle.

M said he was not the kind her daughter would marry. Tashi wanted to know if rain had harmful elements in it. M said decent girls stayed clear of rain.

When it is hot, undress in the dark. Go to the roof. If the monsoon clouds appear, wish farmers well.

Mothers teach their daughters to pick the best tomatoes. Shy to the touch. Surface of cement. Tashi asks if husbands are picked the same way.

Sunspot on cheeks. Wash with rose water. Pluck under your arm.

S held his penis and ran around the tree saying he was blessing it. The elder roared with laughter and said he would grow up to be a "wild" one.

S was blessed. Free from the cycle of female births.

M taught us to peel an apple without disturbing it, saying time and again how important it was to concentrate on the knife.

This is an example of a good woman:

Hibernation

Grass was refusing growth in eastern Tibet. The rainmaster struck his damaru, lay his cheek against the river and called for rain.

M said life too was a matter of preparation and adjustment. We lit butter lamps at the stupa and watched a trickle of light gather on the Buddha's eyebrows. Butter smog as air.

The Tara statue had tears in her eyes. The caretaker produced the piece of scrap paper he had used to wipe it off. Words ran into each other where water touched ink like meandering veins in a frayed wrist. The monk blessed himself with it as I read:

100 kilos of sugar
100 packets of Taj Tea.
Total = 2,000 rupees.

For days people stood in line to give offerings to the statue. Prayers fell as the spine of streets were wet for weeks. M kept us close to her, burned incense all day and said something was in the air. Water continued to thrash the gullies.

Mosquitoes chewed the night to pieces. Then sunlight.

The elders said the chief oracle of the Tibetan government in exile had predicted we were closer to negotiations but he could hear the cries of women slicing the air before him. When he dropped to the floor, he had a hint of a smile. M said no place was safe and offered the first burst of marigolds to the deities.

Very little made sense. News came of a day's rain in the east.

After life. After life. So elders comb their prayer beads.

She is

Her voice is a roundness. On full moon days, she talks about renouncing meat but the butcher has his routine. And blood.

M's wisdom. Still reliable.

There are sounds we cannot hear but understand in motion. Slicing of air with hips. Crushing grass, saying these are my feet. I want my feet in my shadow. Suffice to meet desires halfway.

Quiet. We say her chakras are in place.

When the thermos shatters, she knows the direction of its spill. She knows how to lead and follow. Know her from this.

Sounds we cannot hear. The wind blows and we say it is cool.

Night slips under the door. We are tucked into bed and kissed a fleeting one. Through the curtains, her voice loosens like thread from an old blanket, row upon row. We watch her teeth in the dark and read her words. She speaks in perfect order, facing where the breeze can tug it towards canals stretching for sound.

Her faith abides by the cycle of the moon. See how perfect she is.

The year of the earth rooster

On the fourth month of the new year, we bought one hundred goldfish. One by one M dropped the slippery thrashing bodies into the lake.

We knew our turn would come – new kite, ice cream in the hot afternoon. The places we revealed as nature, mistaken for habit.

The sky unfolding its ocean. Cloud patterns below the blue. The world revolved around us. Trees with rounded heads standing stiff and long.

That was how we learned, prayers before sleep and morning prayers. And at night the moon racing past clouds – a clear path

as though we were watching a movie. The daily rituals and the yearly ones. One year we could not find fish, we were far from water.

I wasn't sure what that meant for us. M found a market of birds and we set them flying near a goddess's temple. Watched them flee blindly, as streets opened up.

We counted the ones who stayed on the ground. M said their past would take them home. The moon was a thin stem but we got our story.

(iii)

The sun on M's oiled knees.
Tea in the garden.
No fault
but a sense of place
is necessary.
And the heart
beats a little
slower.

In between

Late for the feast. Let me guess, she said, everything worked against you.

Some pulverize experiences at the pool. When the air slaps, they flip into the water and speak of the excitations of distress. The stratagems of delivering an annulled emotion. And how is one to read a nod? Is a nod an exclamation?

Does one kiss after a nod? A walk outside. People dusted everywhere.

A woman mutters something about the tea being too weak. The walls threaten to expose us, shadows pinch as we mutter jouissance, jouissance, while the university teacher said the use of the word was a considerable error. A most lamentable error, given half of us are illiterate and unattached. Think of words in their system of birth. Think of primate words in a relationship. Now do you see, the teacher said. Ah, see.

Dogs were barking for no reason.

Some of us went to the ghats and watched the dead burn. Woman in white wailed, her hair a dumb struck line against her rocking spine. We look for other distractions in a place of death.

In the afternoon meanings are extolled.

We are asked to name our loves. I will not, he said, use common language to talk of love. I will not jump into the substance without reinforcement. He took his body to the breeze and swayed till we begged him to stop. The rain subsided but we were still wet.

Thousands have died in a nod.

When birds flew

I take S to the airport. We wave at planes all morning.

He yells out the names of people he knows and is happy to see them leave.

Strangers bend towards each other like branches heaving in wind. A conspiracy of finger trails seal the afternoon.

People with destinations. Cold light breaks on us.

I look for ways to explain parting. Altitude and clear skies make it possible for the iron birds to fly.

We wave to the little windows above us. I blow a long kiss and he laughs.

I tell him what we are seeing is not normal. We should not be in the air. Sometimes things go wrong when we are not on our own feet.

He has seen many crows fall from electric poles and die. He has also seen young girls in the *Diamond Circus* swing from thin plastic ropes in thin nylon suits.

I say in some situations the best you can do is very little.

A couple who survived a plane crash was on a TV show. The man said he saw details of his life swivel before him. He said everything made sense to him. When he said everything, his left hand trembled.

His wife said she tried to pray. She realized all her life she had been praying to someone she didn't know.

Still, she said, the best she could do was pray.

Carried from here

Due to early monsoon rain, Saturday's class is dismissed. Seven nuns abandon their books on the roof.

Raindrops, I say in English. They want to learn functional words: *immediately, enlightenment, conversion.*

A man pisses outside the window. He draws a perfect square on the wall, then sticks his tongue out at us.

Night brings its night talk. Yeshe hides her face behind her robes, asks for a precise translation of masturbation.

Stars are motionless on the street. We squat in the dark and learn to count.

Water drove the dogs crazy. M says it has more to do with the place. Serves dried turnips to the nuns.

I translate letters for parents whose children are learning other things. Unpredictable in his allegiance to English,

a Tibetan son sends orange mountains of love to his mother. The gloaming chews up the horizon.

The nuns want to know if I can teach them what the "school people" learn.

I tell them one learns according to ones needs, as the evening news is read in crisp English.

Doma pines for winter. She has a new woolen sweater, the style not quite nun-like. But she is ready for it.

I wanted paper. Bone white. Cheap Chinese paper, she said as she touched it.

In some sense

Under the throat of a bridge, the exchange of letters. We grow small, we grow small.

Women made ashes of a city. When the enemy entered the gates, they heard flames lick sandstone. Clothes scream for water. A city was burnt by women. Their names translated by General Henry: *Arbor Born. Moon-Glad. Deer.* It was the system of the brown people, he said, that killed their women.

The names stripping before him.

I go through his words and find replacements in another language. Names remain names.

Sun time in the south. Chillum and port. All the hippies complain the naked have no place to go. I am told I do not make a good hippie.

Long life. Powerful woman. The translation of a name.

Mausumi writes from India. She buys beef from the Muslims, pork from the Hindus. She is, she says, the only one in harmony with herself.

Ends letter with a hug from the trencherwoman.

Sliced tongue

Pigeons leave their hiding beds.
The sun does not bring light but it is day.
An hour of day we know as prayer time.
We toss grains into the air,
watch how in timorous light their outline
arrives as motion and thought.
Still, life keeps death. Places called home,
in someone else's country.

(iv)

Snow blessed the fields into a severe display of absence. A crunch of softness under our feet while ahead, a monochromatic luminescence bewilders our eyes.

We do not speak of anything important. We do not ask any questions.

White everywhere, till deeper into its world, we see footprints unfamiliar. When we turn to leave, how the sky twisted. Hoary grass. The sun teases their tops into glistening marble or sand.

Nothing moves. No words appear.

How Thupten comes to knowing

It must depend on methods of knowing. At the first glance consent is rarely the instrument of control. A hand offered is clasped.

When meaning is made, co-exist.

First the construction of an agenda. When walk is mentioned, ask what? Where? How?

If slow, something decent is usually worn. If yes is given. Happily, yes happily the path spits.

(v)

Daisies in the field. A sudden intrusion of light. Crush of wind through hair. No ascent of sight.

Can tiny feet take you far. Deliver you? Some follow that step for step method.

Trim desires and prepare to listen to snow falling at night. Recognize distance through time.

In the opium fields no one is breathing. The pollen raising a ladder to the sky gods.

Water and dust delving deeper. If we could see a destination.

Count the steps

A daughter went to the valley to find death. Mist hung like phlegm. Temple bells brought worshippers with milk and marigold. She went to each house and asked if anyone had seen death. She had been there after the day's duties were stranded; when lotus flowers bundled for the night, a little girl said. She was slices of apple in the sun.

Some women remain daughters; no sense in being anything else if you are good at it.

Women jump into wells all the time. Women also jump into stockings and we watch, announce the best legs to the best legs. 90 women jumped into a well in one village. Three survived: wife, mother, daughter.

Do you know water washes the first time.

F

F had old world habits: a dip in the river at sunrise; tea the colour of rust; fresh bread the way his mother had taught M to make. We cut our lives to meet his habits. M said his first touch had been like a whip from a bamboo rod. She meant it as a commendable fact. When F was kind his face was round, rounder than goblins. When we sent him away in the river, M cried and clung to his dust as though she were clutching at his feet or his hand. Even then, he slipped away.

F's

F feeds pigeons so his son can watch them closely. He knows these
are pleasures he can offer his child. The boy laughs as he runs into
the little bodies and scatters them. He doesn't know this is
happiness. That in years he will think of the day his father led him
through the flying birds, and make this memory sacred. F is
unable to see the small body as a shell. He wants him to never
change. He teaches him words that cannot break: air, angel, fly.
He cannot believe in destiny while he can still give only what he
wants. Snow takes over the streets and he tries not to think about
angels. Death comes easily to mind. To the gods he says, do not
take what is not yours.

A summer in town

All day long airplanes flew in and out of town. We ordered our conversation around their positions in the air.

Our sky was broad and speckled. Mother's belly. Every time we looked up, it stared down at us so inarticulate and dry.

Sky so blue it drew red strips on the necks of the girls, who refused to leave the roof, and waved at planes all evening.

The mountain visitors said they finally saw the life of the town people. We looked around to explain how there was more or less, but it was Sunday and the streets were busy.

Street sounds and air sounds. Silver and black dust flecks fell on us.

M remembers the day through the gold chain around the visitor's hand. Its rush to gold flecks when her arms were in movement.

The words came to us after we put the hands to rest. How the yellow of the bracelet hit our eyes, botanical egg yolk yellow.

Books tell me that was the year the King took a wife.

How rules are made

The silver lining, M said, would come, would come. Some things remained the same: the curtain in the neighbour's house, the one-eyed dog's bark, new hit songs on Sunday afternoon radio programs.

The back of S's throat hid a kernel of some foreign nut and the doctor said, *this is one fine esophagus your kid got there, madam.*

M said S was unfortunate. He was the only one to lose his footing on our maiden river expedition. He pulled himself up by tugging on M's skirt. She lost her toe nail and some skin off her knee.

He lost his share of candy and made enemies of us for the day.

M said S required additional prayers. The rest of us would survive snake bites and food poisoning and hot summers lying on the roof, crying – *ahoy, ahoy* all night at the mosquitoes. The neighbours said they could hardly wait for us to grow up and leave the house.

We were shorter than the other kids. M said it had to do with F's side of the family. Bald and short men all over town were related to us.

The boys wanted to be men. F was not available.

M kissed us on our lips and said she was as good as any man.

(vi)

Breasts do not fulfill hands. The right size depends on location.

Rivers gather what they will around them and continue.

Baby steps adhere to props. Vulnerability, at a certain point.

The gradients of intellect. How eyes adjust to colour. Negative externalities. Question. Questions.

Faith is necessary now: we are fashioned for change.

Blood thickens. There is a possibility.

How Thubten sang his songs

You are adapted to speeches of silence, speak he said, speak.

Magpies shuffled in the neighbourhood as the world opened noisily.
Empty tongues are so heavy, I said. What do you know of life, you
who live in the cave?

Someone was getting married next door. A woman's giggle pierced
the room. The world outside could not be kept out.

He summoned a milkman from the street. What causes you grief?
Milk, said the man, milk.

He said to know where I was, I need to know where I came from.
I could only hear one word at a time.

When I am with people, I am in love with people. When I am
alone, I am alone.

What do you see in a cave when there is no light?

Shadows burn.

Fire.

Fire.

Allowance

Night begins at a national hour. No guardians of the night here, only the belligerent horn of cars shredding conversations so that apologies are made, over and over.

The elders speak of love between mantras. Not coming or leaving. Not blushing but sunk in the fading pink housecoat of a permanent guest.

We must take to each other as window to dust. Eyes of duty; rooted and lax.

Days attended to in uninterrupted vociferosity and still there is no suitable place for grief. Cheeks are the only platform. The elders say it is nothing but expectation that make us weep. They offer no words as sympathy.

Windows shut us against the cold. A summer temperature inhabits the house. No defenses against sleep. No guardians of the night.

News at night

She was in the middle of a sentence when her face went blank. Stranded half-way through the evening news, F regarded the next day with great suspicion.

He called her the newswoman even though her name appeared with her every night. This was her job. And this was the world we lived in: a schedule for darkness.

Thrice a week, our neighbourhood planned for a three hour black out. Planners carved the city into zones. The city took a new shape every night.

Cooks rebelled against menus. Shops drew half their shutters down. Monks escaped from their evening readings and scaled the gates to get some night air. Most of us took to our beds.

The streets' narrow and hesitant black, threw only their smells. Fermented rice on broken glass and, rotting, rotting everywhere, the neigbhourhood altar offerings.

Preparing for the third lesson

Grass was green in shadows. The sun had chewed the colour from the rest of its body. Tapioca rust. Tap water, M said, was for the house and its people.

We waited for rain to take care of certain things.

The flowers got special attention. Small things came first with her.

Our garden was of weed. Her flowers came late and died young.

The grass stayed through winter and cushioned our bottom while M read from books she found in the house. Her breath kept to the slow motion responses of our mind.

One story was of a man part fool, part yearner. The one who burned a house for love and took to raising banana trees. He was the fool in the story she did not finish. He was not from our country. He was not from the country we lived in.

S broke a bit of his front tooth and seemed pleased. M said it was a sign of maturity and suddenly the day seemed shorter. We buried it with a daisy but didn't remember which prayer was appropriate. S had just learned the "Lord's prayer" in school and took the occasion to show off.

Our protectors didn't speak English nor were we Christians. We listened to S, then slept in the sun. Butterflies spread their monster shadows.

Summer days had turned some petals awry. Four flowers bloomed in revolt. The wind blew softly between our ear and hair – its music keen to be noticed.

Laying the grounds

S always got the bone with the marrow. M said he was a boy and needed more to grow. She said "more" in a way that excluded little.

We were habituated to seeing the streets peopled. On some days women walked behind their men.

M was the best mother. She sliced potatoes thin as rice paper and put them over our eyes. She had read somewhere that it was good for eyes. Jetsun corrected her and said it was cucumber, not potato. Potato was potato.

Jetsun had a mole removed from her nose and was considered fashionable.

Seasons dictated our passions. We had summer; we had winter; and the rains fell in between for a long time. It was almost winter so we huddled (like infant mice) up to M.

The streets emptied at nine – as though a giant flush had swept everyone out.

The girls seen after were questionable.

Women walked slower than men, looked around more and stopped periodically. It was a dictate of nature, of difference in form and matter. M read that.

M said certain adjectives were not flattering for girls: shrewd, aggressive, and plain. There were more but these three were to be avoided.

Plain, she said on second thinking, was a good thing, if used by a woman for another woman.

Third lesson

When the elder died in her sleep, Samten was dancing to Nepalese rap under looms suspended at an abandoned carpet factory.

No explanations were made by the Tibetan doctor. Impermanence, he said when asked for the fourth time.

The elders swarmed in grays and browns. Brought rituals to keep his mother's wandering soul in non-life. Too many illusions, they said, in *bardo*.

Food and sweet juniper incense were sent to the scattered mother out in the garden.

No more tears, the lama said. It is the dead who suffer, not the living. He said the departed one's senses were magnified. She wasn't aware of her own death. Think of her living in death. Think of her in her imagined body.

For forty-eight days, Samten lived with prayers and clung to her new birth.

Later he remembered how his body had refused to move at a certain moment on the dance floor. His head, he said, had not adhered to the beat he had practiced to. He was all out of step with his partner.

Now she is dead, the lama said. Do not speak her name out loud. She is now your mother who is no more.

Later he remembered how he loved seeing his mother who was no more with her shopping bag in the market. Always, meat and a bunch of coriander.

Always, a magenta umbrella folded in her hand.

Later he remembered the largest pieces of meat were given to him.

How M ruled the world

At the last minute, the picnic was cancelled. No reason given but the look on M's face. The sky, she said, was coming down.

We watched dust eat dust and foraged for purple glass marbles. A rubber slipper opened out its lizard tongue.

The food on the kitchen table was meant for open air so M was cooking something else for dinner.

All day we waited for someone to come through our gate.

A beggar was ignored when he refused bread. He wanted money or clean clothes.

M had boiled ten eggs so she made us eat two. Cut in the center, half-white, half-yellow, they looked like owl eyes. Mid afternoon, the sky was so silky, we thought she'd change her mind.

We built stupas out of pebbles and rearranged the flowerpots in alphabetical order. Marigold, nasturtium, rhododendron.

M said she had always been afraid of having kids. We didn't know if she meant us or the pots. She pointed to our faces but we were still laughing.

We lay against her stomach. Heard rivulets roll.

She let us listen to her heart. Our M was a drum machine. Thud. Thud. Thud. Thud.

Storm

The night ends with warnings.

Lock the door. Draw the curtains.

Pull the blue dress down to knees.

Ankles. Up beyond shoulders.

Dry crackling cotton.

The places that make you

are those spread far from you.

Look around. Here is where you break.

Here is the place allowing you to slide off.

Off from where you began.

Entry

In trust, we begin.

A grandfather: bald and short.

A father: bald and short.

In the beginning we use family as lineage for there are places still where the longer you go back, the stronger is your bone.

Maybe I mean to tell you instead of the day we ate peanuts on aging grass and watched shells settle on clean shoes.

Sister. Sister, come wrap your wound in mine.

We are framed for departures we are never prepared for.

Walk here. Into this assemblage. Into this alley of slippery language.

Passage

Fifty horses were lost with my grandfather. They are of the other world. Still, M said, they too died.

This is the way we know our history: a great grandfather poisoned at nineteen. A grandfather shot to death. A grandmother who was beautiful and also shot to death.

At the discovery of the word *patriotism,* S distends like sparkles on tin roofs. Tomorrow, and yet tomorrow, he says, he will march to liberate his country. I tell him it will come to no use.

I am the pot with a hole and water flows out of me. I cannot be firmly concentrated and loosely relaxed.

M knows people are killed, (some are born into it). She also knows what colours worked well on her mother.

She says nothing about the past. Says I have her beautiful mother's calves. Or what is remembered of them.

Intersect

The wives were home when the photo was in progress. They selected the shirt, cleaned the brocade trimmed boots, then called for tea as the men coughed dust over the plains.

Rustle of deep purple silk. Signature of self. Men too must have their walk.

The photographer insisted on the sun as a backdrop, for its stretching habit.

Women had their walk. A particular hesitancy was detected in some of them which led to stray stitches in hemlines and a stated idea of womanhood.

Shuffle of paper beneath skin. The creation of soil under feet.

The Mishmi Hills Monar sings a willy-nilly tune. There is no way to tell who sings more sweetly. The male has florescent bronze-green, or blue plumage.

The female is ordinary, as is expected in the mountains. Draped in brown like widows separating rice from stone. But this is now.

We don't ask how their women died. The men were in prison or in the fields. They were on their feet. They are recalled by other men.

Let the dead stay in their world, the women say. They are remembered for their sons.

When clouds are distraught, they rock their grief and rivers amble at their pace. Fish go where they can. To the west or south.

Many gather at the river bank and raise their voices as hammer to rock. Prick the sky, they pray.

But what do most of us know of the man who brings rain to the earth.

(vii)

Roses in the room,
sky falling in angles.
Twenty elephants
have left her chest.
So little said, but the deed
done. How vultures in some other place
were offered and they ate.
Rivers under all surfaces.
So is built.
Immense. Savor.

Of forgiveness

Hashish and wild daisies covered public land. S discovered that, combined, they made a striking bunch. M said the green had an unleafy smell but it reminded her of a certain purple flower in Tibet. At night the dragon sent his breath into the sky.

There are more colours than we see. S creates names for those left out of his colouring book.

Every time we visit the local art shop, M rushes to a painting where a bald head rests on a stream of mucus and blue water. Too much unexplained pain, she says. She cannot see such a horizon for a monk. We tell her it is the sea monster who comes alive on full moon nights and forgives all mischievous children.

Red is blood. Red is the colour of M's cheeks when she laughs.

When S was four, his forehead hit a rock as he greeted the milkman who apologized as he took S to the hospital. His responsibility had not been to distract.

The doctor sang tribal songs as he washed the wound. Some specificities prevail.

M took S to the rock and said he would heal if he sat on it for an hour. She said all wounds began in redness but were harder to wash away with age.

She said the scar on his forehead became him.

Leh

The lines on Jetsun's palms have changed and the palmist is not able to translate them without reassurances. He says he sees a long life ahead.

Jetsun says she is to die at 50: a family tradition.

At 17,580 feet above sea level, she grins into a camera. The sky fleeing from her.

Here are people who cannot adapt to change. After marriage they are given a new name. But mothers continue to press old names.

We look for the Old Fort Lane. You mean the lane behind Pasang Tsering's house, a man says.

The stupa sits on precious relics no one sees, but we take our prayers around it. A tourist asks how we can presume faith in stones painted with limestone. The facts, he says, are missing.

We tell him he could die in an hour.

As expected we feel lost here. Alleys alter on paper. No indications of how sunlight will fall on stones and patterns of piss. The map cannot lead to our destination.

We take a wrong turn and come upon ruins. Patches of sun on our forehead.

A monk emerges out of the corridor and asks if we want to visit a shrine from the 10th century. Only men he says.

Across, a dog licks his swollen sex, then creeps close to my feet.

I count the years on his head. Feed him the stars.

Member

Halfway through our dream, M woke us up. She wanted to show us where the secret stash of money was, in case, she said, something happened to her.

S suggested she show us in the morning. It was dark outside and he had cold bones. M said morning was hours away and it would take time to get there.

She wasn't old like some mothers. She wasn't sick. She was just always thinking of things that could happen.

Every day could be an end, she'd say, as though stray mutts would take over the government. We were instructed where to go if anything happened to her and F. We were not citizens of the country we lived in, nor did we have refugee papers. M wanted us to belong to a place.

One day, she'd say, she'd buy a lottery ticket. Nobody had won in our town for ten years. M said lottery hawkers were all thieves. She never bought a ticket. Said there was already too much in life that needed hope.

She wrapped her money in a handkerchief and hid it in a shoe. S thought it was an obvious place. She said he was right. It was so obvious no thief would find it.

Crossing eyes and lollipops

Sunset alters the room into a jaundiced pallor.

I have not been here before. But that is not enough to make me a stranger.

The last three men in the park dust their pants and help each other up. They do not look around to check their belongings.

From this distance, they look like little boys crossing the street.

Perhaps they are. My lover cannot see me without glasses.

This evening we do not speak of love. We don't trespass on speech when lips have their duties. The sun sulks a little longer. I wonder if our words carry sense when we are not facing each other. If sentences are distracted by hair and the ellipses of hands.

In a place I call home, prayer bowls are being emptied. The sun makes no display.

Gathering himself, he ambles behind the mountains before dogs assemble at street corners to begin their tasks.

Bardo

A hundred and one butter lamps are offered to my uncle who is no more.

Distraction proves fatal in death. A curtain of butter imprints in air.

After the burning of bones, ashes are sent on pilgrimage. You are dead, go into life, we pray. My uncle was a man given to giggles in solemn moments.

Memory springs like crocuses in bloom. Self conscious and precise.

Without blurring the cornea, details are resuscitated. Dried yak meat between teeth. Semblance of what is.

Do not be distracted, Uncle who is no more.

He does not see his reflection in the river. The arching of speech over "s" as he is becoming.

Curvature of spine as it cracked on a misty morning. A shadow evades the wall.

You are no more, Uncle who is no more.

Every seven days he must relive his moment of expiration. The living pray frequently amid burning juniper.

Communication efforts require the right initiative.

Somewhere along the line matters of motion and rest are resolved.

Crows pick the last offerings. You are someone else, uncle no more.

Summer in Himachal

All along "Lover's Road" monks rested on rocks. It was a mosquito evening.

The tea garden lay like rows of green caterpillars pinned to a board.

S was in the mood for explanations. We had come for the sunset.

To show where we are, we recall where we were the night before. And the night before. Columns stand.

When the sun went down, S flung an inch long stick, dusted his pants and stepped towards the moon.

He floundered a little when I motioned towards him. The show was over. He remarked how it all seemed to happen without ceremony.

The way home was unlit. A year ago two young men had stolen the street lamps for a New Year's Party.

Too bad you weren't here for that, a young man said. Quite a night they made of the demure village.

Porch lights claimed their territory. Red robes led the way.

Tashi

Always returning to night,
between sleep and awareness
a slender moment of life-like drama.
I am not known to wandering men
of mid-night streets, but I would like to
hear what they think of me. The only proof
I exist is because you are not here.
Time is pushing forward, then backward.
The giant bulldozer smoothing the path
so we have one less obstacle.
When you appear, I will fall into a pose.
Read tarot cards and take up mandolin.

The water song

M's mother was so beautiful her father hid her in a box. I choose to believe this version of a story even though reason compels me to question the existence of one such box. Wooden or steel. Details make it permanent.

Cement roofs do not entertain the reality of rain. Only when the curtain is drenched do you acknowledge it.

I am reminded of Jetsun, how after dipping her feet in the Ganges, thought she felt a little flutter in her head.

After my hands are washed, I undo my altar. The offered is erased from my possession even as it remains.

After the dishes are put away, after the curtains are drawn, some women will make love.

It is not the knowing but the moment after saying *ah* that pleases.

A ritual is a place of wisdom. In time you learn how much water exactly fills seven prayer bowls.

Somewhere must be a photo of M's mother. When I see it, I will understand why M never told me she jumped from a bridge and tried to take a Chinese soldier with her.

A lama said I was her reincarnation. I have the same underestimated will. M's will is more flamboyant so it is suggested I learn from her.

Horses, a French man once said, see only one path. He was also referring to me.

After losing an image, you learn to live in sentences.

The new jug for the prayer bowl does not know its own ability to contain water.

Everything is isolated. And dependent.

Before the rain

Four days it rained after she died.

The plants put to bed by her broke their spines and lay flat. Turned brown so we forgot they were there.

Some districts were declared disaster zones. We saw roofs slide down the river and foreign aid arrive on TV; midnight blue blankets and bags of rice.

The world cricket series began in India and a 19-year old made the first wicket. The players wore starched white clothes.

I was comforted with updates on the latest death tolls.

A cow floated down the tumid river from one village to the next without any injuries and was named Karo after the river.

Numbers rose. Portraits of orphaned mothers and children dominated national news. Mourners followed the colour of grief in shades of white.

Three players were out in two hours.

Cremation in the rain allows for little composure: umbrellas not forgotten, extra wood, mud on white.

Throughout the day, transistors carried the score from street to street. One player from the visiting team complained of migraines.

Numbers had risen. On the fifth day, we had sun. Everyone hung their clothes out in their yards.

To understand how we are

In the magazines, our town became a city under dust; its inhabitants hardy, peaceful and leather-like (this is how we read about ourselves).

We were used to dust and its squatting tendencies between eyebrows and toes. No surface in seclusion.

M said she wasn't going to be evaluated by someone who stayed amongst us for a week and thought he knew her. She picked a word from a magazine and tried to fit it on her.

Sometimes we pretended we were tourists in our own part of the city. We carried a camera, looked into little shops that had all the things M would not have in the house. We haggled over prices. Tried silver nose rings.

Said – *absurd piece of jewellery – how quaint – stunning craftsmanship.*

The experience made us feel far from hills and rivers. We had one street that took us out or led us back again into narrow lanes.

The shopkeepers played along.

It was easy to recognize the ones who belonged and those who were just passing by even though dust gathered us equally.

Fourth lesson

Entrusted in your care, the equivalent of speech. The harbor in sea mist if ships come that way.

The oddness of the word "pomade" in a room overlooking a church steeple.

Speech measured by what is within definition.

Certain dates are mentioned as testament to a continuity of self. Still, most mornings pass without coincidences as the day is charted on the way to the kitchen.

The cycle of blood. The flexibility of muscles from intent and inherent traditions. The disciplined desire.

Siberian cranes map their wings towards the Indian continent.

Measure what is made. Its eventual contour.

Initiation

When lightning strikes, it takes a particular body to fall.

The rest become incidents. Recalled to the precints of the body; appropriation in motion. Props and sound.

A man has left medical school and gone backpacking to South America. A man has sent a letter to his love, asking for friendship. Not love.

Without names, any story can be appropriated.

The city undoes himself inch by inch. Divesting layers of fog that we begin to associate with the place. In the end, it is different.

Lightning pixilated through far-sighted eyes. Hazy as stymied tissues.

Under normal circumstances, a man is seen as a good person or not such a good person. These are negotiable.

What we would do for clarity. What we do for clarity.

We are left no choice, but memory persists.

Unbalanced sage

The first sign of aging, M said, when F refused a piece of fatty meat. The dress looked new and clean on her. White daisies on a blue field of cotton and polyester. An inch above her knees. She looked like a thin boy.

We turn her around to see if veins ran their tracks down her calves. Jetsun wanted to see what hers are like. M got a mirror and held it against her leg for a closer look.

We were talking about legs and veins and then of other vertical lines. Tributaries run into the mouth of the river Zachu. What is close to home comes to mind first.

F said moments like this made him feel he was different. M corrected the grammatical composure of the sentence. Soon we were talking about how M was younger but wiser.

We watched F dry his hair in the sun. M plucked gray strands from the top of his head. He wanted more hair and believed two strands grew for each plucked.

F believes anything that cannot be proved.

The sun was throwing tantrums. Everything felt familiar but from the west we could hear drums. M said it was the afternoon news on the radio and she knew the man who played the drums for the music. He had a silver ring in his right ear and read communist books.

F thought gray hair grew thicker. It was the colour that was thicker not the hair. He plucked two out to illustrate his point but the wind was blowing.

The afternoon news came through the air. Then a tale about crossed love.

S and love

The conversation turned to love, as it usually does. We had guests who were older than the young ones and younger than the elders. S was the youngest and he thought he had to grow up to speak of love.

S loved M more than anyone in the world but thought it didn't count.

M said in the end it came down to how much an individual could stay apparent and open. Like a tree. Like the sky. A tulip. S had never seen tulips but he liked the word. Two lips.

M said love was similar to a half-remembered dream. Tulips again. She began to speak of her love for F, then faltered.

Our guest is in love with a girl he met just once. He does not know if she will call. M tells him to prepare for the worst, maybe she lost the paper with his number, maybe the paper got wet and the words are gone. He thinks he wrote it with a ballpoint. Even so, M says. Even so.

Easier to rely on her ineptitude to locate paper than her lack of interest. He feels better but doubts his ability to lure women.

M told us about a man who was afraid because she was too kind to him. Afterwards, she remembered how sweet his smile had been.

The two in love talk about love. How they found it. M said no one ever finds love.

Cars were roaring down the street making the sound of a waterfall.

S said he could recognize people he loved from a distance. He watched the road but didn't see anyone. It was not the walking hour of the day.

(viii)

The fog is a horizon. I draw tiny alligators on the window and pretend to brush clouds away.

You are thin and dark. You must not be happy where you are.

The weather man makes predictions for the next day.

Are you happy? At the tip of the ice berg they say, are hints of clefts and loose water.

Windmills are chipping on a patch of yawning field in a blank postcard.

In the picture you are smiling over a bunch of flowers. Daffodils or dahlias of some kind.

Partial sun

The promise of evening came early every winter. Prayers around the stupa. Love under blankets. Those of us who believed in prayers stayed up late.

Some of us believed in deities. But we felt our parents knew best.

Tashi Restaurant had become *Tashi Tailoring*. The cook had learnt to sew from his grandmother. M said adaptability was something we needed to learn in school.

We were little and had people we wanted to be like, but M said they had no jobs, only capricious hairstyles.

More than once a year something happened that was beyond a collective explanation. A bus fell off the road outside the city. In the struggle to explain what he had heard on the street, S lost a rupee he was saving for the man with the ice cream cart.

M said our city shrank when death came. She would know someone or someone who knew someone on that bus. All day she fingered her prayer beads.

F came home with a few metres of cloth. He said they were new in the market and thought M needed a new dress. M took S and me to *Tashi Tailoring*. Tashi said we were the first customers and children always brought good luck.

The ice-cream man was at his usual spot. S stood still and searched his pocket again. I gave him a rupee. He was the youngest.

Jetsun

Jetsun wore orange like it was an everyday colour. M asked her if she was thinking of becoming a nun and Jetsun laughed. At the end of the street, she blew a kiss. M said her side of the family was not known for their style.

We didn't know where that put us. We were her children and were said to look like her. Then S wanted to know if F had style.

When F laughs, trees turn their necks towards him. M says he has a sometimes style.

We wanted to know if style could be appropriated from distant cousins. We were thinking of Jetsun and how she always got the elders to talk about her. Her tattooed eyebrows. Her crimson nails.

Most of the young girls put red and maroon away from their body.

M's body was flat to view. She was hanging our clothes in the sun and for a moment, she looked like a dancer. Her shirt was brown bordering on red – a red older women declared appropriate.

The sudden analysis of her body made her look most like herself. We debated if her body was considered a good body. She said she was married so how would she know?

We looked for F but he was not interested in our questions in the middle of the day.

He asked what kind of style we were talking about. We didn't know words with multiple meanings.

P with the wooden leg passed by the house. Then the night dogs went mad for the moon.

Hill Station Passages

Transparent, the town smeared itself around nightfall. House lights attempted star life.

There were no rooms on Main Street. No roads bifurcating from it.

A stranger's town can make you shy. Dogs barked at our heels. Avuncular and in their own way, marking every entry.

Here is someone else's place of origin.

Dust in the morning – eager-eyed grit. Amber grass.

People spilled on to the street like red ants driven out of hiding.

Light removed all images of the night. What was visible was not recognizable.

Two lips: summer on our grounds

We stare at Jetsun for hours and wonder what it would be like to kiss her. M says her mouth is a saw.

Stars are unlit. Strangers walk past the night into the next shift of light. The garden is sleepless with nocturnal guests. Damp summer nights and the precision of crickets. We have no choice but to sleep early.

M says if she were a man she would shave her head every summer. S wants to be a jacaranda tree. I state if I were a man I would have only daughters. S says I will be in a position to have as many daughters as I want.

I meant something else but am not sure anymore. Perhaps it has something to do with a story about knights.

Next morning, we wait for the sun. Fog restless as the dogs.

S has taken to gardening. He collects earthworms from the neighbourhood and feeds them into our garden. M wants to know what his intention is. He needs time to think.

M had meant visibility of effort. Flowers? Shrubs? Juniper for incense?

S wants only red flowers in the garden. He has no explanations but an intuition that it will ultimately reap profit. We are not from a business family. M's grandfather was a farmer. M's father had started as a farmer before leaving his land to sew shirts for monks.

M said F's job was something or the other. She isn't sure what he is best at but knows he can coax water through pipes.

It is July. The jacaranda tree enjoys rain and keeps well.

South of the rim

On the first glimpse of the mountain S said it was bigger than he remembered seeing it from his father's shoulders. How as a kid he watched sight fall into the sandy well and understood why some things would not be explained.

When we were there we spoke of other places. Water of emerald sheen. Mynahs.

How the lack of temples suspended the magic. How at some other time at another site we have wondered how it would feel to be here.

The old rocks in front of us had devotees floating in their gloved hands and feet.

In the end it is the familiar that seeks us.

Air rode on phlegm. Snow, further north.

S said he understood why his mother could never stop sleeping with her husband's shirt even after he was dead for fifteen years.

At the bottom of the river might be a stone trying to climb up.

We wanted to bury the image of an innuendo of wind cutting through the pillars.

Red dust stretched into an inaudible pitch.

Leaving

Stupas ratified the road
Rearing its head
As though certain of its fate.
Behind us, rain   (rain dripping)
Descended on fields.
Noses pressed against
The panes.
We watched
The oblique fall of water.   (water fall obliquely)

Three Star Guest House

Lunch was postponed by an hour. Or maybe longer, M said.

The stream was dry and the tall one had yet to wash the spinach.

M said he never paid any attention to her even though he was her cook. Never stored water, never washed when the water was whistling in the yard.

The tall one said the stream was his timekeeper. Only morning duties for the morning.

The water ran through the middle of the garden, then crept under the gate to spill itself on the street. Little lanes were transformed into gushing streams. Like veins in my hand, he said.

M said 4 a.m. was a good time to collect water. Then nothing. Nothing during midday. It was magic, she said.

The next day the stream ran dry in the middle of laundry. We returned to washing at dusk. Nothing was working according to M's plans.

The stream had its own hours. Minutes and seconds, the cook said.

He raised his hands up towards his God, asked if we had seen anything like this.

Worship

Twice, S lost his temper on the way to the temple.

The sun made no excuses. (It was summer.) Women in crimson saris sang before the shrine offering sleepy marigolds and oil lamps to the priest. Their flexing calves led unruly toenails to bow in and out while their feet gave no indication of rapture.

I said the women were dancing.

S said Devi was his favorite deity. She had a perfect forehead. He wanted to know why I did not prostrate. I said I had my own deities.

On the way back he stopped at the stream to wash his neck. This is the place, he said, pointing to his throat, that needs attention. I told him streams rarely wash. I told him streams distribute.

Fireflies were in a trance around us. Water thrashed like blindfolded monkeys.

In the evening I went to the monastery and offered butter lamps. The elder's body prostrated in the regimented order. Her left breast escaped her blouse as she went on her knees.

I thrust his hand away from mine. My hands clutched my hipbones.

The elder looked at my shirt stained with dust.

White was not good, she said, too much washing.

Untitled dance

As the monks stepped out in their masks for the Lion dance, S announced he was tired of trying to understand. *It's a lama dance,* I said. *Watch their feet kick dust.*

You can unravel a complete story by the pressure of feet on shoes.

We do not recognize the masked dancers when the dance is over. Having returned, they are themselves.

In the end I settle for words.

There is a particular message of anger when M rubs her chin. She is rubbing her chin as S tells her he is unable to find significance in bowing before idols.

The trees in the garden send their branches to lean in one direction. The gardener says predictions are made by the self opting for aberrations.

I am taught to accept the visible, but there are possibilities in interpretation.

The full moon labored over the hill, breaking the dark's code. When I turned to show him how a moon too, can appear timid, it had moved.

The ruins complete in its light.

No words passed between us. Vultures overhead were combing.

On the way to the red city

Thirty sparrows formed a circle over our heads. S said we were in a metaphor.

We are divided by two mother tongues. Both nomadic.

He spread the word "vast" between us. I saw the sky as he might have. Mnemosyne and stout desert shrubs.

As looking into dreams and wondering how far we have wandered into sleep.

I said the sky was absent. He said the word absent in another language.

We were in a rush to see a petrified forest caught in sunset. An open sky waited in the approaching evening.

(ix)

Not silent the night.
How across beams
pigeons learn to find rest.
Violets plucked from their beds
on Monday. Or Wednesday.
So little sense and life lived. Life prints
in precise stitches. The effect
of rain. How sleep keeps the night
in and out of view.
How keenly we learn
to breathe if we do.
The white of a gown:
of birch or stone.
And sleep,
sleep, sleep.

Saying it again

I meet her ashes in the monastery kitchen. The cook has adopted a habit of talking to her, believing ears can't be the only funnel for sound. I don't want her to be in a corner but clay jars get cold and this is a warm place.

We play old Hindi songs that recall the ways a heart remembers. *My innocent heart. How can I carry you to love?* I hold her and sit near the stove. She could read life without statistics. The cook tells a story in an unfamiliar dialect. We allow our eyes to follow a happy thin cook and his garrulous parrot.

She did not speak this dialect.

The story concerns love but the cook doesn't know it. It has to do more with the woman who gave the parrot to the cook, but he describes the colour of the parrot for a long time. We understand green and orange by the way his fingers rub his skin. A love story, I say. He says no, I wasn't paying attention to details. It is a story about hunger. How it can change even a parrot.

Same thing I say. Love is born from hunger of the stomach. He says no, love is born from boredom. Hunger is like the sun, he says. Boredom, a slow storm.

She was a good woman. I hear it from people all the time.

When I return, I will build a little stupa for her in the sun. She'll live there. Among other things, she taught me to be good.

Body as what is remembered

The Year 2120. No reason why it should be remembered by a nation except that some lost their mothers. Nations mourn when they are reminded.

Existence is acknowledged when it is visible. Onion stains on breath. Deep coral rib. The place of birth ought to be important.

And would it have been different if the sea had been within normal vision? In the mountains, normal vision varies. Clear days begin on elemental blue. If one insists, there is more to see.

In a region of Nangchen, tooth life is short. Twenty year-olds are known to bare smooth gums.

What if the harbinger of birth was a rooster's shriek? If pink cheeks were not so unfashionable.

The place of death is unidentifiable. But the jackal's night song is noticed.

I am not from the tooth-falling region of Nangchen. But my father is.

Marigolds can be grown in an empty kerosene barrel. Eggs shells and soggy tea leaves applied as fodder.

Rain at an unlikely hour and hips were wet because there was so much bending.

Without a name the story could be anyone's. So there is a second name. And a third for the region you belong to if regions matter where you're from.

What comes out of your mouth is what you become. And if you don't speak, that too is worth noting.

Fifth lesson

At a certain altitude the rhododendron nivale refused colour.

M was not one to share facts unrelated to me.

The women around were married. And then those declared old.

Knowledge comes from what you pay attention to.

Onion stems under the tongue so we didn't waste tears.

Forty was an age that truncated our lifeline. Then these women dressed like sturdy tree trunks in shaded banyan groves.

Then they went around the stupa and gathered for tea at tiny tea stalls.

Wear pink while you can, they said to their daughters. *We should know.*

One more say

Think on this when prayers fall like thick paint on dry asphalt.

Think on this when the face is fading.

Think on this and be decisive in your motions. The breathing. The utterance.

No Eastern star leading conch shells and a rainbow at dusk. Those who must believe, do.

Who dares to question the accuracy of a direction when the journey was not theirs.

The moment of birth. Before the father extended his arm towards the mother.

Here is a location. Here it is scattering like mustard seeds.

PHOTO: Marilyn Kennell

TSERING WANGMO DHOMPA grew up in the Tibetan communities in India and Nepal. She received her MA from University of Massachussetts and her MFA in Creative Writing from San Francisco State University. Tsering is the author of two chapbooks, *In Writing the Names*, (A.bacus, Potes & Poets Press) and *Recurring Gestures* (Tangram Press). Her work has appeared in the *Atlanta Review, Boston Review, Mid American Review, 26, Zyzzyva* and others. Tsering lives in San Francisco.

OTHER POETRY TITLES FROM APOGEE PRESS

dust and conscience
by **Truong Tran**

"Something extremely important is going on,
something wonderful." —Lyn Hejinian

placing the accents
by **Truong Tran**

"A voluptuary of the difficult real. To be entered,
and entered. Gratefully." —Kathleen Fraser

Oh
by **Cole Swensen**

"Oh is opera cool." —Marjorie Perloff

The Pleasures of C
by **Edward Smallfield**

"These are poems of thrilling uneasiness and probing reward."
—Kathleen Fraser

Human Forest
by **Denise Newman**

"Like imbibing a divine elixir, making one realize how thirsty
one has been all this time." —Gillian Conoley

bok of (h)rs
by **Pattie McCarthy**

"This is simply a gorgeous book." —Cole Swensen

fine
by **Stefanie Marlis**

"An etymology of our sexual and physical lives, our unknown lives,
our daily lives." —Edward Kleinschmidt Mayes

Speed of Life
by **Edward Kleinschmidt Mayes**

"These poems are at the harsh center of things."
—Eavan Boland

**TO ORDER OR FOR MORE INFORMATION GO TO
WWW.APOGEEPRESS.COM**